OVER 200
AMAZING
SEX TRICKS
&TECHNIQUES
FOR WOMEN

First published in Great Britain in 2001 by Robson
Books, 10 Blenheim Court, Brewery Road,
London N7 9NY

A member of the Chrysalis Group plc

British Library Cataloguing in Publication Data
A catalogue record for this title is available from the
British Library.

ISBN 1 86105 460 2

Printed by Butler & Tanner Ltd, London and Frome
Designed by Richard Mason

OVER 200 AMAZING SEX TRICKS & TECHNIQUES FOR WOMEN

ANNE HOOPER
AND PHILLIP HODSON

ROBSON BOOKS

Contents

1

Mind Joy

Feel good about yourself

It is difficult to make an intimate relationship with someone when you don't respect or like yourself. Try believing you are:

1. Attractive
2. Interesting
3. Sexy
4. Loving

If you have any doubts go for assertion training, which will help you feel great.

Live in the present

5 The sex that blew the top of your head off yesterday was yesterday. Each day, each love-making session, is new.

6 See erotic fantasy as a gorgeous, life-enhancing pleasure in itself. Don't look on it as a means to an end.

7 Sexual fantasy is a unique sexual experience since it embodies a type of tension that can't be really experienced 'in the flesh'. This tension is also the erotic pull between what may be wonderful for you but bad for others. It represents the balance between freedom of thought and 'repression of the forbidden'.

The top five female fantasies

8 Swimming in a sunlit sea where the ripples of the water and the lapping of the waves induce blissful sensations.

9 The audition where young men are made to show off their bodies as they compete for a starring role.

10 Under the doctor where the doctor takes advantage while giving a routine examination.

11 Riding with the Hell's Angels – a night of initiation.

12 In the gym – a lesbian fantasy which takes place in the locker room.

Make every moment count

When you get used to a sexual routine, what was once new knowledge shifts from one side of the brain into a kind of dull filing area section on the other side. This filing section lets you now function on automatic pilot instead of carefully thinking everything through every time. This means that if you and your partner want to re-capture the freshness of sex you need to work on the ELEMENT of SURPRISE.

Surprising moments

13 Set up his screensaver with a series of erotic pictures of yourself. (Only make sure the photos are ones you wouldn't mind transmitted to the ends of the earth via the Internet.)

14 Leave a suggestive message with his mobile phone service.

15 Plant a love note in the cereal packet.

16 Do something in bed you have never done before (see pages 139 for suggestions).

A surprise only works if it is done for the benefit of the one to be surprised. A surprise is done to make THEM think and feel – not you.

Sharpen your erotic senses by:

17 Closing your eyes

18 Touching yourself

19 Touching your partner but experiencing the touch as pleasure for yourself

20 Identifying and describing the effects of his scent

In Germany 48 per cent of people find their partner's individual scent (without perfume) sexually arousing and 46 per cent find their partner's personal scent combined with perfume sexy too.

Focus on the individual

Try to see your partner as a person and not just as a fantasy figure. This is important when making a sensual relationship but hard to do since we all suffer from the Distorted Mirror effect when we fall in love. Then, we cannot help but see the lover as someone incredibly enhanced.

You might:

21 Look behind your partner's physical face or body and see through to their sexual self.

22 Close your eyes and breathe in your partner's scent. Try the test of imagining they are part of a line-up and you must identify them while blindfolded only by their smell.

23 Think of him and not you. This means from time to time freeing your mind of what you might like to happen to you and truly focusing on what your lover would prefer.

Forget your own reward

24 Do something for your lover with no thought of yourself.

25 Practise scrupulous dental hygiene. The mouth is the first approach point and if you inadvertently pong of last night's dinner you won't smell so good to your man. Sixteen per cent of German men and women admit ted to getting turned on by the scent of their lover's breath but the statistic didn't analyse its quality!

26 Judge yourself by how much happiness you bring your partner.

An altruistic approach is wonderful so long as you sense it is reciprocated. Do not however fall into the trap of letting him take you for granted.

Enhancing sex for yourself

27 When lovemaking, let go of the idea of orgasm as your aim. Instead focus on the immediate sensation and enjoy your sensuality wherever you experience it in your body. Picture an internal flowchart of wonderful circular sensuality.

28 You can get more extraordinary and extreme body sensation over a long period of time by forgetting about orgasm than you can by aiming specifically at it and seeking a quick release.

No need to be lonely

Don't approach sex on the basis of scoring notches in your belt. You will end up feeling empty or very bored. If you find yourself without a partner let yourself follow your instincts.

29 If restlessness pushes you to go out and hunt don't worry about it . . .

30 But make sure you practise safe sex.

31 If your body tells you to rest and wait, enjoy the waiting time and see the value of time to yourself.

Identify your sexual flashpoints

32 A sexual flashpoint can be a thought: for example the knowledge that the minute you meet someone special you want to go to bed with them.

33 Or an urgent desire for sex: women have two special times in their menstrual month when this is highly likely to happen. The first is around ovulation – roughly halfway through the menstrual month and the second is the day before or a couple of days before your period is expected.

34 Observe the seasons. Make the most of spring and autumn. These are the sexiest times of the year.

Whatever your flashpoint may be – once you know it, let yourself enjoy it. Follow it up. Don't resist – except for a first-class reason!

Thought for the day

35 Groom your genitals.

36 'Change sex' for the day.

37 Combine two sorts of bliss – sex and chocolate.

Alter the shape of your mound of Venus

Using scissors and/or razor, you might:

38 Remove most of your pubic hair thus making yourself look much younger.

39 Style your pubic hair into a heart shape.

40 Trim your pubic hair so that it hangs low making you look very well endowed.

Alter the contours of your breasts and navel

Bearing in mind that we must suffer in order to be beautiful, consider seriously the pain of piercing. Devotees of erotic piercing insist that the piercing itself is an erotic event to be shared with the friend of your heart. What's more those diddly twiddly rings and studs make for spectacular sensation during sex. Prime erotic sites are:

41 The nipples
42 The navel
43 The labia

Be a man

Agree with your partner that you and he will change sex for the day. This involves:

44 Dressing in opposite sex clothing.

45 Him wearing make-up and you doing without.

46 Switching sex roles. Think yourself into character and act as it feels appropriate. Women sometimes become amazingly pushy and men surprisingly meek.

Sex an' chocs–aholic

47 Spread a plastic sheet across the carpet, cover each other's bodies in melted chocolate and see who can lick the most off first, without getting sick. Best quality chocolate only. Prize? A choco-orgasm.

The advanced clitoris

48 Get to know your clitoris as well as you know your face.

49 Check it out in the mirror.

50 Watch its colour changes as it gets increasingly excited.

The sexiest clitoral strokes

51 Pull back your clitoral hood with one hand and gently touch the tip of the clitoris. It can feel much sexier done this way plus you have the added advantage of not being able to lose the tip when it goes through one of its characteristic changes of size.

52 Check out a short up and down stroke on the left-hand side. Then compare this with the same on the right side.

53 Practise a light stroke then a hard stroke.

54 Go for twirling on the clitoral head, then around the head.

The vaginal party

Your vagina is about to get a special celebration date. Make your bedroom private, warm, sweet-smelling and comfortable. Your aim is to make your vagina feel wonderful.

55 Explore the outer rim by pulling down on it slightly with one finger. Most women find that the lower part of the vaginal entrance where it meets with the perineum feels sexiest.

56 Treat your perineum to a super Vitamin E oil massage. This makes it supple and helps explore your particular sensitivities.

57 Try putting your longest fingers inside your vagina to find your G-spot.

Gee whiz

Your G-spot (if you have one – not every woman does) will be on the upper wall of the vagina probably a long way back. It helps if you possess long musician's fingers! The latest theory is that it is the clitoral root, the very base of the clitoris. Whatever! It feels like a small swelling.

58 To obtain sensual feeling press down on it with the pads of the finger(s), occasionally lightening then strengthening the pressure.

The three-finger aerobic

59 Push your left hand under your thigh and, coming up from underneath, put your fore fingers in your vagina and pull backward until you can feel the area stretching back across the perineum. With your right hand place your forefingers inside your vagina and pull it up towards the clitoris while your thumb gets busy on a very sensuous clitoral rub. It feels like being (pleasantly) assaulted.

Thumbelina

Let rip with a little thumb work on the erogenous zones.

60 Use the thumbs to twirl around the nipples.

61 Then twirl at the far side of each breast.

62 Then up and down the sides of the breasts.

63 Tucking your hand below your perineum, stroke with the fingers while using your thumb to move rhythmically against the clitoris. It feels like two people making love to you.

The right moves

64 Tell your man that you have discovered several moves that you adore and so that he can get an idea of how sensational they are, you are going to try out their equivalent on him. Then demonstrate some of the moves suggested on previous pages. This way you can give him a treat.

65 Find out how similar or different your erogenous zones are.

66 Teach him, through his own experience what he might do for you.

Anti-shyness tip: if your treat consists of oral sex and you feel shy of doing this to him, spread a little ice cream onto his genitals and then lick it off. You like ice cream. You begin with a pleasure. What starts off as a game can turn into a complete feast.

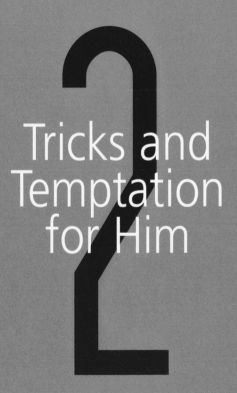

Tricks and Temptation for Him

Give him the three degrees . . . of kissing

DON'T

67 Leap straight down his throat with your tongue – he could suffocate!

68 Smear his face with drool.

69 Breathe pure garlic.

70 Be in a tearing hurry. Slow is not only sexier, it means you don't feel so needy.

DO

71 Kiss him on the lips softly . . .

72 Then firmly and

73 (Not until he is clearly responding), go for HARD. Kiss him on other places such as behind the ears, in and around the ears and generally nibble around the sides of his neck.

Dynamite. Only when he gets really passionate – bite his lip – not so hard as to go through but just enough to give him a jolt.

Eat sweet

The right smell is an aphrodisiac – literally – so work on your diet and on your personal hygiene.

74 Eat pleasant exotic tastes such as cinnamon, cardamom, peppermint, lemon for sexy nights in.

75 Avoid garlic, onions, cheese unless working all week.

Not only does your breath need to smell sweet but so too does your body odour. What you eat gets exuded through the pores of your skin and even if you are unaware, you DO smell of your diet. What's more, when your man works his way down to your genitals, the taste he encounters will be influenced by your recent meals . . . Think about it (or don't!).

76 However, don't wash too much. Your natural body odour is also an aphrodisiac. Remember the Emperor Napoleon who messaged ahead to Empress Josephine to say 'Home in three days – don't wash!'

TRICKS AND TEMPTATION FOR HIM

His secret trigger points

77 The inner nerves. Feel for the space underneath the penis head, at the end of the frenulum, and press. This point is dynamite.

78 The coronal ridge. This ring-like ridge around the head of the penis is packed with nerve endings and some men can get off from stimulation on this area alone.

79 The perineum. This is so much more sensitive than most people expect that you can orchestrate the entire excitement/orgasm sequence from here alone. You can begin arousing him by softly stroking this area of skin between the root of the penis and the anus. You can rotate the pads of your fingers on the areas nearest the penis root and nearest the anal opening, and build up excitement. And, if he promises to come far too quickly, you can block his orgasm by pressing very hard with your finger on the point halfway along the perineum, between the anus and the scrotum. If you press hard and firmly enough you literally block the ejaculate, prevent orgasm and your man is then free to carry on with his work in your good cause.

Groom his genitals

This sounds as if it ought to come in the preliminaries part of this book but the experience of having someone trim and shape the hair around his most private parts is deliciously erotic. There's something about the cold tingle of steel and the brushing of casual fingers around his most sensitive parts to get the imagination – not to mention the erection – up.

80 Tell him that you are going to transform his appearance. When you are done his penis will look longer! He probably won't object. You manage this by clipping the pubic hair above his penis so that a diamond shaped space (pointing upwards) appears above his penis. Then go for the sides of his pubes, trimming these so that they are wide at the top and narrow at the bottom where they meet the scrotum. The difference is startling.

81 A good reason why many women are nervous about taking the initiative with their men is they don't really know what they are supposed to be doing. We rehearse for practically every other situation and there is absolutely no reason why sex should be an exception. Find yourself a small cucumber or a large zucchini/courgette, scrub off all traces of pesticide and begin.

82 **Oral sex.** Gently slide your lips over the cucumber and avoid munching. The way to ensure that your teeth do not take a casual bite is to try to wrap your lips over them as you go down on the little green fellow. You can let the lips relax on the upward move but re-wrap next time you go down. Practise a soft slide, a firm slide, then a downright mouth clamp.

83 Try taking the cucumber into the front of your mouth, then the back of the mouth – experiment with how much of it you can comfortably suck on before getting unable to breathe. Let the saliva flow freely.

84 Special trick. As you slide backwards and forwards practise flicking the underneath of the cucumber head with your pointed tongue. If this were a real penis your tongue would catch on the frenulum.

Massage tricks

All massages need to start off with an all-over body massage. But sooner or later your man is going to nudge you in the direction between his legs. Here's how you can offer your cucumber an amazing experience.

85 Holding your cucumber with the left hand, place your right palm across the 'head'. After every up and down of the left hand, circle the right hand lightly on the head. As the bottom hand goes down, you bring the top hand up. Next you take the top hand down at the same time as you bring the bottom hand up. These two moves constitute the main stroke.

86 The twist. Same as the previous stroke only you twist each hand slightly.

Condom tricks

Practice makes perfect. Hold the condom in one hand, by the tip, squeezing it so that there is no air in the tip. Never unroll the condom in advance. Hold the penis near the head in the other. Your cucumber has the advantage of always being erect. Your man doesn't so you do need to ensure he is aroused before clothing him in rubber. Now place the rubber on the cucumber head and, curving your fingers slightly, unroll it and push it down. When carried out well, this can be a continuous flowing movement.

87 **Oral condom wrap.** Clamping the tip of the condom in your mouth, position it neatly over the head of the cucumber, then let the rim of your mouth unroll it down the cucumber shaft. Remember the tip of wrapping your lips across your teeth so that the condom avoids perforation. This takes a bit of rehearsal.

88 **Something for madam.** All this rehearsal can be exhausting. When you've finished, consider rewarding yourself by checking your powers of vaginal enclosure. Imagining that your cucumber is alive and attached to a scrummy man, exercise your vaginal muscles on it. Once you've made the fit as tight as possible, use your best finger to play upon your clitoris so that you can make your cucumber feel more of a happy vegetable by giving you an orgasm.

Exquisite penis torture — **suck on a lemon/munch on a mint**

Anything that gives your guy a novel sensation on his favourite body organ goes down well.

89 The acid from natural lemon juice, or vodka.
90 The tingle of minty toothpaste.
91 The less stingy mint mouthwash.

Process these in your own mouth first and then lovingly apply them during oral sex.

Hot tea and cold ice cubes

92 Heat up the inside of your mouth first with a gulp of hot tea. Apply mouth to penis. Pause for a minute and munch on an ice cube. As soon as possible, so that your man can be shocked by the contrast, apply mouth to penis again. Take hot and cold in turns.

Wash him with gritty skin scrub

93 Coat your hands with the gritty mealy skin scrub that is often used to help remove dead skin. Holding his penis gently, roll it backward and forward between your two hands.

94 At a later stage in the proceedings slide the tip of one finger or two into his anus, while operating on his penis either by hand or by mouth.

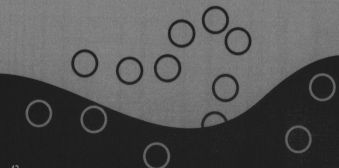

Ayurvedic honey bath

95 The Ayurvedic massage treatment owes a great deal to the amazing sensation of warm oil poured exquisitely all over you. In this variation, and only when swathed in towels or plastic sheeting, pour warmed (but not hot) melted honey over his genitals. The secret to the amazing sensation is to get a small but steady stream coming continuously. One way of doing this would be to put the honey in a sturdy plastic bag and pierce a small hole at the bottom Once the honey has coated his thighs, your task is to lick it off.

The sensuous penis bath

96 After all the sensuous juices and substances have been rubbed in or licked off, it's time to bathe your man. Take him back to the days of childhood by telling him that he is not to lift a finger. You are going to be his hand (and body) maiden. After you have run the bath, ask him to sit on the edge with his feet in the bathwater. Gently soap his genitals, paying attention to every nook and cranny. When you have done as much as possible, ask him to sit down now in the bath and continue to stroke and clear his skin under water. Slide his foreskin back and clean underneath. Don't forget that soap stings so go easy on its use. Don't forget that his perineum and anal passage will need attention too. Make your hand strokes like a slippery, slidy massage.

PhD in penis pulling

97 **Scarfing.** If you've tried stimulating your self through a layer of fine silk or chiffon, you'll understand the impact of this one. Wrap a flimsy scarf around your loved one's proud penis. With your hands on the scarfed area use a gentle up and down motion, twisting occasionally. You can either move the skin under the scarf or you can move the scarf itself. Each offers a separate experience. Practise on your own fingers or genitals first to get the idea.

98 **The jelly trick.** This is for dedicated games players only. Fill a condom with as much sloppy jelly as it will hold, then fit it. Even though much of the jelly will be displaced, some will remain. Holding the condom tight at the top to contain the jelly, slide the other hand up and down his penis. Warm jelly offers a very different sensation to cold jelly.

99 **The count down.** Pour on tons of lubricant. This penis massage consists of two strokes. First grip the top of the penis with the left hand and place the right hand underneath his testicles with the fingers pointing towards the anus. As you slide the left hand down you bring the right hand up. You aim for them to meet somewhere around the base of the penis. The second stroke reverses this in that now you slide the left hand back up his penis and the right hand back down towards the anus. The key to a really sensual experience is to do the two strokes regularly and steadily. Then do the sequence ten times, then nine times, right down to one stroke only.

100 **The pulsar.** Clasp your two hands around the head of his penis. Squeeze gently, hold for a second then let go. Pause. Then do it again. The trick is to imitate the rhythm of his pulse. When done during ejaculation it can be fantastic. Time your pulsations to go with his contractions.

Did you know that the male orgasm contracts at 0.8 second intervals – exactly the same as those of the female? Time it.

The peaking trick

101 Every time you sense your man is nearing his point of no return, stop genital stimulation for a while and focus on something else. Then go back to it. This is the concept of peaking. The more stopping and starting you do, the more peaking he will experience. The long-term benefit – his orgasm will be far more explosive.

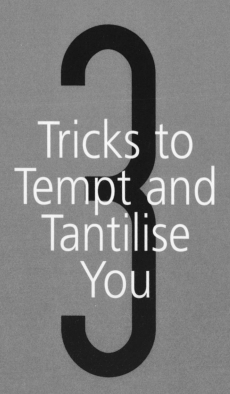

3

Tricks to
Tempt and
Tantilise
You

Sensation boosters

102 If you get TOO tense, bearing down (literally pushing out your genitals as in a bowel movement) helps to de-stress you.

103 If you reckon your vagina isn't getting enough sensation, cut down on the lubrication.

104 Did you know that Eastern women believe that a dry vagina gives their partner a better experience of intercourse?

105 If you are getting excited far too quickly tell your partner you are dying to do oral sex on him and withdraw.

106 If you want to improve the strength of your orgasm go for the stop-start method of 'peaking'.

107 Testosterone is responsible for sensual strength and expression. If you want to make the most of your natural testosterone, use only barrier methods of birth control that do not interfere with your body's natural hormone balance.

108 Consider wedging a vibrator next to your clitoris next time you make love. It works for both of you.

109 Recent research shows that the female genitals, the clitoris, labia and vagina, all get an erection during sexual excitement.

110 Did you know that women in the later weeks of pregnancy are walking around in a permanent state of 25 per cent arousal? This is because their bodies retain more fluid.

111 In the early weeks after giving birth, women's breasts get so engorged that touch can be experienced as painful. Lovemaking goes better if the breasts get left out of things.

112 If, during intercourse, you want to climax without masturbation, ask your man to help you here. Every time he manually stimulates you to a pitch of arousal ask him to stop just that little earlier each time. In theory, you could eventually do without the masturbation altogether.

113 If you adore combining masturbation with intercourse however, enjoy, enjoy!

114 If you want to speed up orgasm, try clenching your buttocks, thighs and vaginal muscles, then letting go, regularly.

115 Did you know that some women can climax through flexing their vaginal muscles alone?

116 A few women experience their first orgasm accidentally by leaning against the washing machine while it is working. The vibrations of the goddess of hygiene get to them!

117 For a really sensational self-stimulation experience, try pulling down on your vagina from the rear while touching yourself at the front.

118 To heighten the rush you get from sex, try doing it with your head hanging over the side of the bed.

119 **Sex trick:** coat yourself liberally with massage oil before making love. This will allow you to slip and slide over and under your man. It also helps your nipples avoid catching in his chest hair and pulling. Some men are sensitive souls!

The clit kit

The clit kit. Extraordinary former call girl Xaviera Hollander writes about what she describes as her survival package. She keeps alongside her bed:

+ A box of paper tissues
+ Lubricants for anal adventures and body anointing
+ Body lotion
+ Vaseline
+ Her contraceptive
+ Rubbers for him
+ A vibrator
+ *A History of Western Philosophy* (you can never know too much)

Xaviera Hollander's girlfriend keeps a string of sturdy beads on her bedside table. She greases her lover's anus with cream and inserts the beads as far as she can. As he is thrusting she pulls them out, one by one, in time with his lovemaking. Then, when she wants him to come, she abruptly jerks the rest of the string, giving him a thundering orgasm.

The facts of life – female style

120 To get the most out of sex you need to give yourself permission to luxuriate in physical pleasure. One woman did so by telling herself that she was a princess and as such entitled to enjoy any luxury or spoiling that she was offered.

121 Women are 100 times more likely to be affected by sexual smell as men. Men, on the other hand, react more negatively to strong perfumes. Trick here: lay off the scent yourself but encourage your man to wear it!

122 On the other hand, men are statistically more likely to be turned on by what they see, by the visual impact of long legs and high heels, the slick of shiny tight trousers, the curve of a rounded bottom.

Trick: women could learn from this by training themselves to notice the sexier points about their man. Men's buttocks are one of women's first focus points!

123 According to the Hite Report for Women, around 30 per cent of women can climax regularly through sexual intercourse alone but around 80 per cent can manage it regularly through masturbation.

124 According to the Kinsey Institute only 23 per cent of younger women regularly experience orgasm but by the time they get past the age of 30, around 90 per cent of them do.

125 The average female orgasm lasts for 21 seconds longer than the average male's. (And still women don't get equal pay.)

126 A small survey showed that out of 12 per cent of women who had yet to experience orgasm, six per cent of them managed to do so after training classes.

127 Women discover masturbation at a later age than men.

128 On the other hand, 3 per cent of women can fantasise to orgasm.

129 Between 10 to 20 per cent of women report having an orgasm in their sleep.

130 Nearly four per cent of women report having a lesbian experience at some time in their life. Lesbians are the least promiscuous group of all humans.

131 Lesbians spend literally hours more on each other's body during lovemaking compared to heterosexuals.

132 Do not worry if you find yourself equally attracted to women as you are to men. US sex researchers Masters and Johnston found that there is a group of men and women who are genuinely attracted to either sex and that these individuals find it normal and natural to fall in love with either men or women. Bisexuality is not abnormal.

The man inside the woman's body

133 Testosterone is the natural hormone that affects a woman's sex drive. Women who experience a sharp rise in sexual desire shortly before a period is due are likely to possess a <u>high level of testosterone.</u>

134 Women in the high testosterone range have the greatest levels of sexual arousal and maintain this arousal for the longest times. They also experience the highest frequencies of sexual fantasy.

135 Paradoxically, high-level testosterone women have less satisfactory love relationships than women with low testosterone.

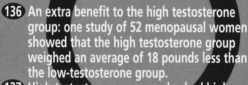

136 An extra benefit to the high testosterone group: one study of 52 menopausal women showed that the high testosterone group weighed an average of 18 pounds less than the low-testosterone group.

137 High-testosterone women also had higher incomes!

138 Another study where single women were given testosterone replacement therapy showed that several dropped out, finding themselves <u>unable to cope with their increased levels of sexual desire.</u>

139 Testosterone replacement can now be easily prescribed since it comes in gel form, which is rubbed into the skin therefore by-passing the liver and getting directly into the blood stream making it safer than before.

Women who find it difficult under normal circumstances to experience orgasm would be sensible to get a blood test to analyse their natural testosterone levels. If these are low, prescribed testosterone can improve:

✦ sexual desire
✦ sensitivity
✦ experience of orgasm

Improve your climax

The tension that leads up to orgasm is experienced all over the body. Climax itself relieves a lot of this but a sudden cease fire of sexual activity can leave a woman feeling strangely unsatisfied. You can improve your orgasmic ending after self-stimulation by:

140 Fitting your hand snugly down over your pubic mound with the fingers curved round inside the front of the vagina and simple pull up against them. You do not slide your fingers but just exert a steady pressure. If you like you can actually throb your fingers in time with the remaining contractions.

Some women find they can prolong their orgasm by deep pressing for many more contractions than they previously thought possible.

141 Many of the suggestions in this section would also be well carried out by your lover. Remember, your lover cannot know what you personally like unless you tell him. He is not a mind reader. You need to find the courage and the technique to ask him to do the things that you love.

142 **Sex trick:** Preface your requests with praise. 'I love the way you stimulate my clitoris. It's marvellous. Please could you keep your hand firmly on my clitoris when I climax so that I can experience all of the climax.' And when he concurs, tell him afterwards, 'That was the longest orgasm I've ever had.' He'll soon get the hang of it!

Your man needs to know:

143 If you like a soft or a firm touch.

144 If you like your vagina stimulated.

145 If you like your clitoris stimulated (who doesn't?).

146 If you like your clitoris stimulated on the left side?

147 Or the right side?

148 Or on the head?

149 If your perineum is sensitive?

150 What you feel about penetration from the rear?

So let him hear it as it is.

Faking orgasm

Don't! It teaches people how NOT to satisfy you on a regular basis.

Basic instinct

151 Women with a high sex drive discover orgasm by basic instinct much as men do. But women with a medium or low sex drive may have to teach themselves.

152 As many as 90 per cent of women eventually get to reach orgasm by some means or other.

Bliss from a bottle

153 Some women find their sexual response is improved by taking Viagra, the male impotence drug.

154 The makers of Viagra are working on a female version, a Viagra update.

155 Health food enthusiasts swear by Ginseng.

156 Wine enthusiasts point out that two glasses of wine loosen inhibitions and make it easier to respond sexually.

157 Sex doctors now know that the drug phentolamine works on the brain's inhibitor centre to loosen up inhibitions and therefore allow desire to come through.

Sexy check list

You and your partner might like to:

158 Vary your lovemaking techniques.

159 Prolong your love sessions . . .

160 But include more 'quickies'.

161 Use a personalised lubricant that becomes associated with your relationship.

162 Rent an X–rated video from the top shelf.

163 Visit a sex shop together.

164 Look at men's magazines, read mutual erotica.

165 Make love in unusual places, i.e. in the garden, on the roof, on a picnic in the woods.

166 Explore your G-Spot.

167 See if you can bring him to orgasm by testicle stimulation alone.

4

Getting
Raunchier

Kundalini meditation

168 Practitioners of kundalini yoga use a special 'opening up the body meditation' before meeting their lover. Divided into 4 parts, you can:

✦ Stand in one spot, with your knees bent. Let your whole body shake, so that it lets go of any tension you might be feeling.

✦ Dance, letting your body flow naturally to the rhythm of the music you will have put on before starting.

✦ Sit, and watch your mind at work, as if it were a film and you were viewing it.

✦ Lie down, and sense the support that the ground offers you.

Tricks you can turn

169 In the red museum. You are an exhibit and your dream partner is blindfolded. He has to identify you through caressing your naked body and you cannot move, regardless of where he touches.

170 The rape of the seven veils. A beautiful slave is brought to the auction block swathed in cloaks and scarves. The cruel slave master slowly peels these away as he describes exactly what he plans to do to the slave. Beneath the cloaks are many thin veils. For each veil that is ripped off, the slave is ravished in some terrible manner.

171 Butterfly kisses. You are naked and forced to lie down in a garden full of flowers. Next you are blindfolded and your erogenous zones painted with a syrup and water mixture that attracts butterflies. Now you have to guess whether it is your partner or a butterfly who touches you. For every wrong guess you are lightly chastised. But with each wrong guess the chastisement gets tougher! Beware of beetles and cockchafers!

172 Star stripper. On a clear night you go out to view the stars. When you return indoors, you must identify ten of the constellations you have just seen. For each mistake you must do something scintillating and starry to your partner.

173 The photographic model. Your poses get more and more extreme until finally you are forced to have sex with the photographer 'for the sake of art'. See the Antonioni film *Blowup* for inspiration.

174 The high-class hooker. You ask your client to tell you exactly what he wants you to do to him. Every time you finish one activity you must ask for the next command. You continue until one of you can go no further.

175 The detective trail. Invite your partner round and leave a trail of clues (such as a red rose, a black condom, a lacy bra) so that he ultimately finds his way into your chamber.

176 **In Transylvania.** He is the vampire and you are the victim. His task is to seriously arouse you by making love to your neck only. He is allowed to suck, nip, lick, tickle, breathe, manipulate your head and neck and to thoroughly restrain your body. (Biting by negotiation only.)

177 **Fair Exchange.** He is allowed to make love exclusively to your breasts provided you are allowed to make love exclusively to his buttocks and back passage. You each take a turn for the other and accept whatever the other chooses to dish out – including orgasm.

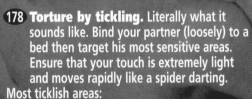

178 Torture by tickling. Literally what it sounds like. Bind your partner (loosely) to a bed then target his most sensitive areas. Ensure that your touch is extremely light and moves rapidly like a spider darting.

Most ticklish areas:

✦ Feet
✦ Belly
✦ Armpits
✦ Inner thighs
✦ Around the breasts/chest

179 Play at pornographers. If you have your own video camera and PC editing suite, make your own 'blue' movie. Then watch it together from your bed. A word of warning. If there is any likelihood your partner is not trustworthy, don't do it. Intimate photos have been known to show up on people's computers on the other side of the world.

180 The quickest. Time your partner (stop watch in hand) to see how fast they can race to climax. Then take your own turn. Make a prize for the winner.

181 The slowest. Time your partner (stopwatch again) and see how many hours sex can be dragged out for. Then take your own turn. Prize here is a good sleep.

182 **Erotic postcards.** Document your love affair with shots of your sexiest moments but make sure neither of you can be identified in the pictures. The challenge is to invent the sexiest postcard to be carried safely in your bag.

Warning: sending matter of a sexual nature through the mail is an offence in certain countries.

183 **Erotic magazine.** For intelligent, well-written but off the wall erotica, think of subscribing to the *Erotic Review*. For a free peep at the mag go to www.eps.org.uk

184 **Erotic reading.** There are two excellent web sites, which provide high quality erotic stories mainly, but not exclusively for women. These are www.erotica-readers.com and www.cleansheets.com

GETTING RAUNCHIER

185 **Please Daddy, tell me a story.** Reading aloud in bed is an erotic art, presently undervalued. A 10- or 15-minute story with a romantic/erotic build-up can feel scintillating. Look in the back of our book *How to Make Great Love to a Woman* (Robson Books) for short story material.

186 **Show me a movie.** Going to bed with your television set has a lot to be said for it. A really sexy movie like *9 1/2 Weeks* or *Betty Blue* can sometimes get so exciting you find you have missed the end of the film.

187 Hello Mum. Sneak up on your fellow while he is talking on the phone to his mother or his bank manager and give him a surprise erection. He'll either love you or kill you.

188 Sitting in the backseat. Drive out to a secluded place where you cannot be overlooked and move to the back seat. In spite of the inconvenience and the cramps the sheer unfamiliarity of the surroundings gets you moving at up to 100 m.p.h.

189 The double ring. Ring his penis with your thumb and forefinger and use the rings to firmly run up and down his penis, first together in the same direction, then apart. Then round and back while still moving up and down. Finally round and back while moving in opposite directions.

Sexual healing

Did you know that according to the ancient Chinese theories of Yin and Yang regular sexual intercourse massages acupressure-type meridian points on the inside of the vagina and the outside of the penis. But to make a thorough difference to your partner's good health you need to practise the Sexual Sets.

190 The Sexual Sets. The sets depend on a series of deep and shallow thrusts of the penis.
You might start with:
✦ 6 shallow and 4 deep
Then go to:
✦ 5 shallow and 5 deep
✦ 4 shallow and 6 deep
✦ 3 shallow and 7 deep
✦ 2 shallow and 6 deep
✦ 1 shallow and 7 deep

Then work your way back in the opposite direction.

Orgasm frequency

Yin and Yang believed that it injured your health to experience too many orgasms. One guideline went:

Age 20	Twice a day
Age 30	Once a day
Age 40	Once every three days
Age 50	Once every five days
Age 60	Once every 10 days

If you feel unwell these frequencies should be cut down by exactly half.

Sex in the summer time ... and in the autumn too. Sex drive differs according to season says Yin and Yang teaching. In China these were the perceived sex frequencies.

Winter	Once every 30 days
Spring	Once every three days
Summer	Once every 15 days
Autumn/Fall	Once every 15 days

Sex in the third millennium. Based on perceived sexual wellbeing that correlates to ancient hibernation habits, men and women are perceived as having in:

Spring	High sexual energy
Summer	Low sexual energy
Autumn/Fall	Rising sexual energy
Winter	Low sexual energy (i.e. sleep!)

191 The joy of shoes. Did you know that one of the real sex differences between men and women is that men get turned on by what they see? This is why they only have to glance at a pair of high heels to get hard. So even if it ruins you, invest in a pair of gorgeous, spindly Manolo Blahniks – Sex in the City style.

192 Stockings too, preferably with seams, add to the illusion of flawless but flashy legs and in case you think this is exaggeration, some men genuinely like being walked over in the spikiest heels imaginable. So next time you come out of the bathroom, keep on your lingerie and stockings and heels, ask your man to roll on to his front and walk up and down his body, taking care to keep your weight off his spine. Make sure he can see what is happening in a floor-length mirror.

193 Big lips. It's a myth to think that pulling fellas ends at the age of 45. One 50-year-old was quoted as saying 'I know that if I put on a short skirt, high heels and bright red lip stick I can have any man in the room.' Lip enlargement is one of the first 'improvements' made by movie stars. Just check out the before and after pictures of Elizabeth Hurley and Julia Roberts. Huge difference!

194 Big suggestions. Why the mouth appeal? The glossy, pulpy look of luscious lips puts the erotically sensitive male in immediate mind of your other lips – the hidden part of your anatomy. Let him see your mouth stretch and smile. And Drew Smith, author of *Rude Sex* insists that a pointed tongue, especially when it happens to be licking a penis, is one of the sexiest sights ever!

195 No bullshit. Although it's true that all these sex tricks can turn your man on, their impact also depends on your state of mind. If you are dressing and acting sexy because your man turns you on like nothing else, that's brilliant. There's nothing quite like the exchange of incredible sexual attraction. If, on the other hand, you don't really fancy the man you are manipulating, it shows. And although he may be attracted, if you are not, what is the point? Never function on automatic.

196 **A rubber erection.** Sexual pioneer Tuppy Owens (of The Outsiders Club) has devised The Rubber Wall, which she erects at her famous Sex Maniac's Ball, an annual event in the UK. The Rubber Wall is a large sheet of translucent back-lit rubber, which you can dance against and slither around, moving against bodies doing the same thing on the other side. You might erect your own Rubber Wall and with a copious supply of glistening, gleaming oil, tell your man that as he gyrates on his side, several women will be pressing up against him on the other side. Now it's your chance to break out into multiple personalities.

197 **Who wants to be an exhibitionist?** Sex
tricks for the show-and-tell show.

✦ Recline on a bed in front of large mirror.
✦ Look at yourself in the mirror as you begin
  to touch your labia and vulva. Watch your
  face as well as your hands. Watch your
  arousal build. If you want to thrust, do so.
  Don't act to the mirror. But exaggerate your
  movements – it will turn you on more.
✦ Invite your partner to watch.
✦ Invite your partner to take part.
✦ Dress up for your mirror. Oil your body.
  Groom your man. Tell yourselves you are
  doing this for a Live Sex Show.
✦ Enjoy, enjoy!

198 **When your sex trick falls flat on its . . . face.** Hopefully you will be so tuned into your partner that you will instinctively know what turns him on and what does not. But women can't always be mind readers (though they are pretty skilful). Sometimes your trick will fall flat. Instead of taking this as a failure, tell yourself instead that you need more practice. So that you can get to know him better you might ask him about:

♦ His earliest sexual experiences.
♦ His family memories of love and affection.
♦ What he learned from the playground.
♦ What he's learned as an adult.
♦ His sexual failures.
♦ His sexual successes.

Practice makes perfect.

5

Vibes, Tubes, Pubes and Lubes

Vibes - the very latest models

There's a small revolution going on in the sex toys industry. Vibrators are being transformed as a result of the fabulous new materials now available. They are soft, malleable, feel like real skin in fun materials such as see-through translucent jellies and are in gorgeous jewel-like colours. Here are some of the best taken from the top vibrator website on the Internet. www.goodvibes.com

Vibes you might like to buy him

199 Cyberskin Vibro Sleeve. A stretchable sleeve made of cyberskin that fits over the penis and includes a vibrating egg for stimulating the sensitive head of the penis.

200 Ball stretcher. A comfortable strap that wraps around the top of the scrotum and is then tightened. The 8 oz weighted bag attached to the strap pulls down the testicles making for surprisingly prolonged sensation.

More vibes
for him

201 Neptune ring vibe. This is a tiny vibrating dolphin attached to a cock ring. This works either by giving your lover a solo buzz or by stimulating the clitoris during intercourse.

202 Gummy Bear ring. A jelly rubber cock ring, which fixes at the base of the penis (or dildo). The blue model comes with a mini-probe for focusing on the G-spot and the red model comes with little side flaps that tickle the clitoris.

Vibes for both of you

203 The Hitachi Magic Wand is still the Rolls-Royce of vibrators. This enormous 2-speed mains-operated model possesses a sturdy wand handle and a huge vibrating head. What is new about it is that there are now attachments fitting on to the head that focus on clitoral stimulation.

VIBES, TUBES, PUBES AND LUBES

204 Acuvibe. This is similar to the Magic Wand but with re-chargeable batteries which last for a good 20 minutes. If you hate all those trailing wires this is the model for you.

205 Dr Scholl's Deluxe Wand. Dr Scholl has graduated from sandals and is now selling his own version of the Magic Wand.

206 Attachments. What is special about the last two vibrators is that there are some cute pink or purple G-spot attachments that can also be used to give your guy a prostate massage. One has a slender curved tip specially shaped to give maximum pressure on the front wall of the vagina where the mysterious female G-spot is located. A red model comes with little side flaps that tickle the clitoris.

207 Relaxus Rechargeable. This is the most powerful battery vibrator of the lot. What's more the rechargeable batteries last for 60 minutes. If you get off on a really intense stimulation, this is the one.

208 Coil operated vibrators. These are the more old-fashioned shapes that look a bit like unwieldy handguns. The Windmere and the Wahl possess the great advantage of being much quieter than most other large vibrators.

Warning: most of the older vibrators are maddeningly noisy. But they are still the fastest, most intense and most effective. One 1970s calculation had it that there is a maximum oscillation (vibration) speed needed for women to be able to reach orgasm. This means that if a vibrator's battery is wearing down you may suddenly find it much more difficult to come.

Contemporary vibrators

209 **Natural contours.** These are small non-phallic shaped vibrators designed by women's soft-porn film-maker Candida Royale after she got thoroughly fed up with the design of the old-fashioned male-inspired sort. They look like 'objets d'art' in candy colours and are small enough to fit into the contours of your hand. Your great aunt might never know what they are for!

Pulsating vibrators. The very latest models don't just vibrate. They do a lot more beside. The key difference is: they pulsate, which many women recognise to be integral to their style of orgasm, especially for G-spot stimulation. They are a lot quieter.

210 The Pulsatron has seven different speeds, throbs and pulses.

211 The iSurge Vibe has five variations, which include vibration, pulsation, escalation and rollercoaster.

Glow in the dark

212 Pretty in Pink is phallic shaped but consists of a series of graduated beads, the largest at the bottom tapering off to the smallest. Made of pink jelly rubber, it is Soft. And Firm. And Very Quiet.

213 Pretty Kitty is a silicone vibrator shaped like a kitten which when used upside down vibrates the clitoris while probing (with Kitty's tail) the vagina or the anus. Nicely quiet.

214 Flex-o-Pleasure consists of a slim handle, a long thin shaft headed by an angled vibrating head. If you like extra stimulation during intercourse this is the perfect one.

Finger vibration

215 **Fukuoku 9000** is one of the most ingenious newer vibrators. Working off tiny watch batteries it fits over your finger like a tiny finger sheath and vibrates. There is no battery pack and no cord. Brilliant for surprises during intercourse since it is virtually undetectable. The kit includes textured rubber pads to fit over the device so that you vary your finger sensation.

216 **Pocket rocket** is a small rocket-shaped vibrator – a little like a pocket torch in appearance. But what transforms it are the wonderful jelly rubber sleeves that fit over it. Comes in lustrous edible colours such as blueberry, grape, lime, strawberry and tangerine. You can also add jelly rubber sleeves shaped like a Bunny (with extra long ears!) or a variety of nubbly textures.

The Japanese school of vibration

The ancient Japanese considered it taboo to make sex toys resembling human genitals so dildos were carved to resemble living creatures. This tradition has lasted through to the modern version of the dildo – the vibrator.

217 The Famous Rabbit Pearl. This consists of a rabbit head – a mid-section of tumbling pearls that create a unique scintillating sensation against the walls of the vagina at the same time that the rabbit ears flutter the clitoris. Made of translucent pink vinyl.

More Japanese vibes

218 Silver Pearl. This has a sci-fi appearance with a rotating shaft, a strong clitoral probe, while the silver pearls in the middle speed along a track to provide a rolling sensation in the vagina. Controls are on a lighted display so that you can adjust in the dark!

219 **Pisces Pearl.** Green or lavender fish-shaped vibrator with fishy clitoral probe and revolving mid-section of stimulating plastic pearls.

All these vibrators can be obtained from www.goodvibes.com but if you prefer to buy in the UK please see page 139 for all addresses.

A round peg
in a . . .

A new London erotic emporium was born when Ky, its proprietor, first tried (with a friend) to buy a strap-on dildo and harness. She was amazed at how difficult it was to find what she wanted and developed the search into a capital-wide survey of sex shops. She also felt uncomfortable in the sex shops and put this down to their being very male-oriented. The end result was the creation of Sh! – a genuine sex boutique for women. Strap-on dildos in her shop are best selling items and in accordance with her customer's needs, she also sells a variety of anal toys. Sh! is at www.sh-womenstore.com

Sh!'s anal creations

220 Thai beads. A string of three small pearly-pink beads to be inserted into the anus and then pulled out slowly, either to accentuate stimulation or in a rush, to heighten climax.

221 Jumbo beads. A graduated larger version.

222 Jelly beads. Spongy ruby equally sized jelly beads with a ring pull that offers a jelly-like sensation.

Butt plugs

Butt plugs are designed to be worn for the feeling of fullness. They are made in silicone or rubber and are easy to clean. Sh!'s butt plugs come with heart-shaped bases and apparently the silicone is excellent for transmitting vibrations – all you have to do is apply your vibrator to the base.

These plugs come in a variety of shapes and sizes. There is:

✦ The long, thin, pointed plug
✦ The shorter, fatter, slightly curved version
✦ The small, squat, fat beaded version

Hands free

223 The double delight. A variety of two-ended dildos to be worn either between women or between heterosexuals when the man enjoys anal penetration.

224 The scissor dildo is a double dildo shaped like a pair of scissors that enables you to penetrate your partner with particular flexibility.

225 The mini-hummer offers targeted vibration for women who find it hard to come. You wear it strapped in place over your clitoris, held on by an elastic waist strap and leg straps. Can be worn during inter-course.

More hands free

226 **Venus Penis.** This is a curved jelly butterfly shape with an integrated dildo so that you can enjoy a spot of penetration as your buzzer stimulates your clitoris.

227 **Triple Stimulation.** This is a cock-ring with a flexible dildo for anal penetration while your man is also penetrating your vagina in the time-honoured manner.

All Sh! Products can be viewed on www.sh-womenstores.com
See page 139 for address.

Lubes

Passion8 is a particularly well-run and discreet sex toy supplier which operates entirely by mail order. The lubes it sells are the wettest and juiciest.

228 Sylk. Tasteless, odourless and non greasy, Sylk mimics the natural vaginal juices. A free sachet is available for sampling. Especially important, Sylk is safe to be used with condoms.

229 KY Jelly. That great old stand-by. It's excellent for use with sex toys and pelvic exercises. But not to be used with condoms.

230 Platinum Wet. This is a top quality US lubricant made by Dr Johnson. It comes in a sexy black bottle and stays wetter and slipperier for longer than any other lubricant in clinical trials. For use by men and women, it's oil free and may be used with condoms.

231 Spike – anal lubrication. Also by Dr Johnson, this comes in a concertina shaped squeeze bottle with a long probe applicator for delivering deep inside.

200 All Passion8 products can be viewed on www.passion8.co.uk. For address see page 139.

232 Senselle. Made by Durex especially for women with lubrication problems. This is my own personal choice – not least because you can buy it over the counter at any good chemist/pharmacist.

VIBES, TUBES, PUBES AND LUBES

Fun lubes

Lubricants come in dozens of flavours and colours. Try edible lubes, small gelatine filled capsules that you bite on during oral sex to flood your partner's genitals with sweet-smelling edible gel. Or chocolate flavoured gel. Or a row of little gelatine pots for flexibility of selection. There are so many different sorts that you are best advised to search two main sites for suggestions. Go to www.annsummers.com or www.goodvibes.com. You can use lubes to spice up the greatest blow job of your man's entire life or to flood in your vagina at the moment of penetration.

Trick: if you are vaginally dry please don't lose sight of the fact that this may mean you are not feeling emotionally safe with your partner. This means that you would be wise to work on making the relationship more intimate before going on to sex.

The goody bag

These days it's getting positively normal to spice up the bedroom with toys. Ann Summers, the British high-street sex shop chain, suggests:

- Handcuffs, in both black leather or pink and fluffy
- Self-adhesive diamanté tattoos
- PVC blindfold
- Kinky heart-shaped bottom paddle
- Fur collar and lead
- Nipple chain

Restrain yourself please

Sh! women's store also suggests nipple clamps and any number of sinister looking restraints. Several US erotica companies revealed that nipple clamps were at the top of the bestselling lists last year. Addresses on page 139.

233 Equipment includes:
+ whips
+ canes
+ paddles
+ cat o' nine tails
+ tackle for tying your partner to the bed, or padlocking him to the furniture

Something for madam

Skin Two makes exceptional clothes out of rubber and PVC. They are slick, shiny and skin-tight. They are also beautifully cut, immensely flattering and stunningly erotic. In fact, they are actually works of art. Address on page 139.

The PVC comes in several new textures. As well as the original PVC there is a realistic leather look, a matt version like unpolished rubber, snakeskin and a slinky sensational satin finish. The clothes include:

234 Gorgeous basques and bodies.

235 Catsuits and dresses with keyhole cut-outs over the breasts.

236 Glossy, shiny military dress, headgirl's dress, maid, nurse and dominatrix dresses, all in glorious shiny shimmering rubber or PVC. (PVC now has its environmental critics but remains fully available.)

Sexual electricity

There's the electricity that sparks between you and your man. But there's also the sort that uses Faraday electricity and bombards him with safe, low voltage, mini-lightning bolts. Many of you will have heard of TENS machines, small box-like objects used in physiotherapy which by pulsating a tiny electrical charge into the skin, relieve physical pain.

237 The sexual version of a TENS-like machine is The Violet Wand. It's been on sale since the 1930s and is presently enjoying a resurrection of interest. It operates by sending sparks through a single electrode and creates an incredibly array of sensations. When held near your body it sends out a continuous stream of tiny lightning bolts, and gives off a distinct purple light. Try kissing while plugged in – better than any spark from a hotel carpet!

Available from www.stockroom.com/sec0506.htm are several sex toys that use the Faraday principle. There are electrical:

238 Butt plugs,
239 Cock rings
240 Vaginal shields

There is also a book entitled *A Guide to Electrical Sex*, which is the first of its kind to explain the Faraday sex phenomenon.

Safety first -
the rules

- ✦ Never do anything to anyone against his/her will.
- ✦ If you are in doubt, ask or don't do it.
- ✦ When playing games of restraint devise a safety word, which will be strictly adhered to.
- ✦ If instinctively you do not trust someone enough to want to play sex games, respect your inner judgement and suggest instead that you and your friend spend more time getting to know each other.
- ✦ Ask about AIDS exposure.
- ✦ Practise safer sex (see pages 133).
- ✦ Do not do anything that would harm any one.
- ✦ Practise birth control.

Sex for One –
Your Body
as a Sexual
Instrument

Play upon yourself as if you are a violin . . . !

241 **Go bathing.** Arrange open-ended time when you can luxuriate in a sweet-scented bath, surrounded by glowing wax night lights, with sensual music playing. Privacy is important. Luxuriously soap yourself with the latest exotic moisturiser and let your hands glide over your slippery body. Don't forget to include your genitals and spend as long as you like, provided you remain warm.

242 When you emerge from the bath water, using one of the new intensive Ayurvedic oils, anoint your body lightly, omitting only the genitals.

See www.momentum98.com/masoils.html or www.nealsyardremedies.com for a wonderful supply of natural flower fragrances with safe, healthy oil bases.

243 Make your bedroom a pleasure dome. Treat yourself as an honoured guest. Prepare your bedroom, so that it is clean and tidy, lit with scented candles (as many or as few as you like) and warm. Place some flowers where your eyes can easily fall on them and make it comfortable.

Above all, arrange some warm, fluffy towelling on the bed and place, by the side of the bed, your massage oil, a packet of tissues and your favourite sex toys. Your aim is to enhance the atmosphere, visually and tactilely.

244 **Pleasure yourself.** You think so highly of yourself that you are prepared to make yourself the gift of an hour's precious time. During that time you are going to pamper your body with the most sensational self-massage you have ever enjoyed. You are a queen who is entitled to body pampering. You slip and slide and glide over every seam and nook in your soft and creamy skin. You are going to touch:

✦ Your face
✦ Your chest
✦ Your abdomen
✦ Your genitals
✦ Your legs and feet

245 **Search out your hot spots.** Your pleasurable task is to touch and tantalise all areas of your body to register your own particular hot spots. Every woman is different. Every woman's eroticism is personal to her and unique. Where one person may get incredibly hot from having her nipples twiddled, others get the sensual shakes from walking spider fingers across the lower abdomen.

Tactile trick: experiment with grades of touch, from quite hard through to fairy light.

246 **Hottest spot of the lot.** Although we vary in our type of response to clitoral stimulation, most of us would agree that this is the sexual power station. Your task now is to experiment with the sort of sensation that your clitoris enjoys. Just as you have searched out the erogenous zones on the rest of the body, now you not only locate your pleasure places but you are encouraged to build on the sensations you find here. Once more experiment with different pressures.

Tactile trick: many women say that the area to the left of their clitoris (as they look down) is the most sensational.

247 Know your clitoral tip. Is it small or large? Is it easy to view? Or hidden away in the folds? Does it erect easily? Or does it take time before it slowly responds? Take a look at it in the mirror. Pull the pubic mound above it right back to expose it. Try the trick of stimulating it while watching yourself in the mirror. Do your genitals change colour as you get aroused? When you get ultra excited, does it strangely seem to disappear? Follow it through as it sinks back into your engorged labia. Keep on stroking. When you have climaxed watch what happens to your clitoris in the mirror.

248 Know your anus. If you are brought up in the UK or the US you have probably been taught that the anal opening is dirty and basically a taboo area. Mainland Europeans however have a more realistic attitude. They are used to regular bathing (in bidets), to inserting gelatine suppositories to aid excretion, even to taking the temperature with a thermometer there.

It's good to reach this degree of comfort with your anus so that you can feel emotionally free to include anal stimulation with great sex. How could you stimulate it?

- ✦ Bathe it.
- ✦ Stroke it.
- ✦ Rub your finger around the outer rim
- ✦ Stretch that outer rim a little.
- ✦ Slip your finger a little way inside and push. Try to enlarge the opening slightly.
- ✦ Push 'around the clockface' – on the hour, quarter, half and three-quarters position. Each provides a different sensation.

249 **Know your orgasm.** Now include anal stimulation with one hand (from underneath) while you focus on clitoral stimulation with the other. You are likely to find that the anal stimulation heightens excitement and turns you on. But don't let yourself come too quickly. If you sense you are about to climax, halt the sensation for a short time. This delays proceedings and allows you to grow even more aroused next time.

Tactile trick: this sequence of stimulating then stopping as you near orgasm is called 'peaking'.

250 **Orgasm options.** How many different sorts of orgasm can you have? There are short ones and shallow ones, long ones and intense ones. There are orgasms that barely ripple, and orgasms that cause a cataclysm. What's more one person may be capable of feeling not just different lengths and strengths of sensation but may also experience orgasm in several different sites in the body simultaneously.

Tactile trick: did you know that when women are pregnant they can feel the ripple of orgasm right across their extended uterus?

251 Take a candle (just make sure it is snuffed before using it as an extension of your probing fingers). Women who find it difficult to turn on at their own touch discover that touch by an object is quite different. It can feel as if a third party is involved, especially if you close your eyes and dream of a useful object like Colin Firth or Hugh Grant. Some women enjoy having the candle inside them, others prefer it as an extended finger, putting in useful homework on their receptive clitoris.

Tactile trick: if candles don't do a lot for you substitute one of the new jelly dildos or even one of the fabulous new vibrators. See page 139.

252 **Daring Decisions.** If a feeling of fullness is vital to your experience of a really fantastic orgasm consider investing in:

✦ A large dildo or vibrator

✦ A butt plug (buy the correct size for your level of elasticity)

✦ One of the Japanese double or triple vibrators where just about every orifice you can think of is thoroughly stimulated.

See page 139.

253 **Germaine Greer's words of wisdom.**
Australian feminist Germaine Greer wrote a
famous book in the late 1960s called *The
Female Eunuch*. One of it's most daring (and
meaningful lines) was: 'If you haven't ever
tasted your own menstrual flow, then sister,
you haven't lived!' Think about it. You
expect your man to be comfortable with
your bodily juices. But don't you think you
should be comfortable too? Tricky but true.
Women don't become instantly poisoned
when they try this experiment.

254 Fantasies, fantasies. You can try every sex position you can think of, including dangling from the ceiling but if you don't bring your fertile brain into play, you may not manage to become aroused. The brain plays a surprisingly large part in turn-on. Long after the sex hormones have quit the body of the older woman, her imagination is still capable of arousing and bringing her back to climax.

If thinking of your present lover doesn't quite do it you might consider dreaming of:

✦ Colin Firth and Hugh Grant (already mentioned).

✦ Being the temple victim inseminated by the sinister warlock.

✦ Ravishing a beautiful young man in the woods.

✦ Riding a powerful motorbike that heats and vibrates between your legs.

Safer Sex

AIDS

Unless you know that you and your man friend could not possibly have been infected with AIDS because you are both virgins, you need to take precautions against contacting this deadly sexual disease. This means protecting yourself by using condoms, avoiding a lot of casual sex and avoiding rough sex that might break your own or your partner's skin.

AIDS stands for acquired immuno-deficiency syndrome. This literally means breakdown of the immune system. You can only get it if you have contracted HIV first. HIV stands for human immuno-deficiency virus. This is caught through unprotected sex, sharing needles if you are a drug addict, and occasionally via a blood transfusion.

Putting on a condom. There's a right way and a wrong way and your condom application matters. That's because there is a tip on the end of each condom that must be pinched to keep the air out of it since if you put the condom on while the air remains inside it stands a good chance of popping thanks to the hearty battering it will receive.

Do not unroll your condom in advance. Holding the tip in one hand, fit the condom over the head of your partner's penis and with the other hand roll it down in a tight fit. Only when the condom reaches the bottom of his shaft can you let go of the tip. Otherwise it will probably fall off anyway.

SEXY BOOKS

How to Make Great Love to a Woman by Anne
Hooper and Phillip Hodson (Robson Books,
London, 2000)
How to Make Great Love to a Man by Phillip
Hodson and Anne Hooper (Robson Books,
London, 2000)
These are twin full colour manuals that detail the
differences and the similarities between men and
women and explain how to make the sensual
most of these.

Real Sex by Grub Smith (HarperCollins)
Extremely funny, over-the-top laddish book by a
columnist for FHM. While getting you to howl
with laughter it also tells you some super-
practical sex facts, such as how to make love to a
sofa. No kidding.

The Penguin Atlas of Human Sexual Behaviour by Judith Mackay (Penguin, London, 2000)
This is a series of maps of the world, each one detailing some aspect of sexuality such as female genital excision, sex tourism, the economy of sex, even a sci-fi style future of sex.

Sexual Healing Through Yin and Yang by Zaihong Shen (Dorling Kindersley, New York, 2001)
Whether or not you are a believer in ancient Chinese methods this provides a fascinating alternative view of how to use sexual intercourse to heal everything from flu to a rash under the left breast. Different.

Sex – the Good Web Guide by Matt Blythe and Jenny Blythe (The Good Web Guide, London, 2000).
An enterprising list of some of the many sex web sites to be found on the Internet. Had you heard of Eros Village? Belly Magazine? Clean Sheets.com? There's a whole new world out there.
Sex Tips and Tales from Women Who Dare, ed. Jo-Anne Baker (Hunter House, London, 2001).
An original and refreshing collection of real sex tales from real women who were unafraid to explore sexual extremes and, surprise, surprise, live to tell their tales. Good value.

SEXY WEB SITES

Sex aids
www.goodvibes.com
www.sh-womenstore.com
www.annsummers.com
www.passion8.co.uk
www.stockroom.com/sec0506.htm

Massage oils
www.momentum98.com/masoils.html
www.nealsyardremedies.com

Fabulous rubber, leather and PVC clothing
www.skintwo.com

Good sexual reading sites
www.cleansheets.com
www.nerve.com
www.eroticaforher.com